A Journey of Love

R.L. Cunningham & Nancy Zitko

authorHOUSE®

AuthorHouse™
1663 Liberty Drive, Suite 200
Bloomington, IN 47403
www.authorhouse.com
Phone: 1-800-839-8640

First published by AuthorHouse   10/10/2008

ISBN: 978-1-4343-8481-2 (sc)

Library of Congress Control Number: 2008905092

Printed in the United States of America
Bloomington, Indiana

This book is printed on acid-free paper.

This book is dedicated to all the pets that we've come to know in our lives. There are so many, and they are all so special in their own way. But I have two special dedications Ozzie and Kodi. We miss you and love you.

Preface

As I sit here at my desk I'm reminded of the constant love that I receive from my pets. It's a love that they give unconditionally. I'm not a very religious person but I'm a very spiritual person. I believe that is this type connection that we have with our pets. So often we take them for granted, but when you take the time to look into their eyes you can feel the connection, and it's extra-sensory. How many times have you thought to yourself, that you know exactly what your pet is thinking? I really believe you do. In planning the idea for this book it also reminded me of the love that I feel for my pets. And as you look around and talk with people or notice how they are interacting with their pets, it shows how much we love them. My journey on these pages will be an introduction to my loved ones and how special they are; I'll speak of people I meet along the way and the little things they do to show their love. The second part of this book will be Nancy's journey of love. You will get to read our journeys from two different perspectives.

I've always loved animals. I've had my share from fish, dogs, cats, birds, and yes, even the little pink, yellow, and blue chicks that you could get at the 5 and 10 years ago. But like most of us it took me years to understand that pets are really a part of our lives, not just something we have around the house. And that understanding came mainly through education. That education was achieved through many ways. But the most important thing that was ever said to me came by way of my best friend, Nancy. We had become involved with the local humane shelter. We began by rescuing a few dogs and cats. One day in conversation, when I guess I was a bit overwhelmed I said "Nancy, we can't save them all." Kneeling down and picking up a little kitten, she looked up at me and replied, "But we can try." Those four words were so profound. It has made such an impact on my life, and it is constantly echoing in my head. "But we can try." Anytime that you ever doubt your reason for doing something, utter those four little words, and hopefully they will spoke the volumes that they spoke to me.

Not all the stories in this book have happy endings. You may experience some sadness, and you may even feel angry. I guess that's the reality we are faced with, but hopefully after reading these pages you will see that our pets are truly masters of love, and that they make our lives a little richer and a little more worthwhile.

His Journey

About Him

It's funny that when I went to write this book I thought I had everything organized only to find out that I was all over the map. I gave the first forty pages to a friend to read and he suggested I tell you a little about myself.

My mother and father were from small bordering towns in Pennsylvania. My father was a steelworker and my mother was a housewife. After my father's untimely death, I was raised by my mother and grandparents until Mother remarried, at which point we moved to a larger city. It was a pretty nice life for the most part, except that my stepfather was the typical mean stepfather. I was thrown out of the house at the age of sixteen. At the age of eighteen I met a girl and we had a child, Robert II. Shortly before Bobby's first birthday his mother abandoned him and I took on the sole responsibility of raising him. I may have been the original Mr. Mom. At times it was a struggle but I loved him very much, and we made it work. He is thirty-seven years old now and we are still together. My life has been enriched by his presence and I wouldn't change a thing.

Several years later I met a woman. I was working in a small jewelry store when she came in from the rain. I went home that night and told a friend that I had just met the woman I would marry. A year later that became a reality and the next ten years were the best times of my life at that time. Her name was Joyce and we also had a son, Christopher. Because Joyce was an officer in the U. S. Army we traveled extensively throughout the states and europe. It was a very interesting and fulfilling time for both of us. During this time I put myself through college studying art, majoring in photography and design. One of my professors whom I admired immensely was Joyce Tennyson, a well known and prolific photographer in her own right. After graduating from college I took correspondence classes from the Institute of Literature. It was after completing this course that I had my first magazine articles published. They were travel articles about Germany. That was over twenty years ago, but my passion for writing has remained.

Since then my life has taken some twists and turns. Joyce and I divorced and then I met Nancy who is also the co author of this book. Hopefully you will learn more of our lives as you travel with us on our journey and how we came to be involved with all of the animals that has crossed our path.

My First Pets

Sandy

Sandy was my first dog. She was a sandy colored cocker spaniel. I was very young, probably five years old. I have only one memory of Sandy. I was playing with her in my backyard under the big maple tree. It must have been fall because the yard was filled with leaves, and I can vividly remember jumping and throwing leaves around while Sandy was running with me. Then one day my mother told me that Sandy was sick and had to be taken somewhere to go to sleep. It wasn't until years later that I discovered what "going to sleep" meant. But I've always hoped that she would still be playing in the leaves.

Pastel Chicks

I'm in my mid fifties now, and years ago, the local 5 & 10 stores had little pastel colored chickens for sale at Easter. You could find them in blue, pink, yellow, and green until, of course their colors eventually faded to white. I don't know how much it cost, probably twenty-five cents, but every year we would get two chicks and put them in a box with a screen over it. We would place them in the pantry, and it was really a lot of fun to play with them. When they got older we would move them out to my grandparents house. They had an old chicken coup where they would live out their days. Of course, as I got older I stopped getting the chicks, and the government stepped in and deemed it was an illegal practice to sell them. But it was a pretty cool memory, and one that I am sure some of you might share.

Jerry

Jerry was my first rescue, although at the time I was only nine years old, and I had no comprehension of rescues. As I said earlier, my mother had remarried. I was soon to find out what type of a person my stepfather was hidden under the smile and presents. One day a stray dog appeared at the porch. He was a little cutie, white with brown spots. He was most probably a mix breed, but at that time he was referred to as just a mutt. I named him Jerry after my mother, and we had lots of fun playing. He showed up in the summer, so I spent lots of time outside with him. He wasn't allowed in the house so he slept on the back porch. Then one day I awoke to find Jerry gone. My stepfather decided that he didn't want me to have a dog, so he supposedly took him to a farm and dropped him off. I was never allowed to have pets of any type after that until I eventually moved away to be on my own.

Sheva

It had been sixteen years since Jerry had been taken from me. I was living in Alexandria, Virginia and a friend of my neighbor had several puppies he was giving away. Sheva was a Shepherd Doberman mix. She was eight weeks old when we picked her up. From the time we acquired her she was a fantastic dog. She was very smart and silly at the same time. One day I left a plate of cookies on the dining room table. When I came back, I found Sheva on top of the table with an empty plate beside her. We also had two cats at that time, and they all got along. Sheva loved to mimic the cats, such as cleaning herself with her paws. We moved quite a bit back then as a family, but when we had to move to Germany for four years, we found it extremely difficult to take her along. Since my stepfather had recently died, and my mother was alone, we decided that she would take care if Sheva until we returned. For four years it was very difficult to not have her around, but she was great company for my mother. When the day came that I arrived back in the U.S. I couldn't wait to see Sheva again. The moment I stepped into my mother's house, it was as if I had never left. Sheva ran up to me and almost knocked me down. I grabbed her and gave her a big hug and she returned with tons of kisses. Sheva lived for over 16 years and finally her cancer became so severe that she had to be put down. This was the second time in my life that I had to deal with the loss of a pet the first one was of course Jerry. But I was considerably older now and it just seemed much more painful. I took her to the vet and said my good-byes. My only regret was that I didn't stay with her until the end. I will never forgive myself for that selfish act. She had always trusted me up until the end and I feel that I let her down. Since that time I always stay and hold them until they are gone. It's a very painful experience for me, but I know they feel comfortable and happy with me by their side.

Pumpkin & Tiger

P umpkin and Tiger were my first two cats. Pumpkin was a calico and Tiger had long golden hair. Both were females. Unfortunately, for my first animals I didn't have any education on how raise a pet. As they got older I would let them outside, and of course due to my ignorance, they both became pregnant. Pumpkin had three kittens, and Tiger had four. A funny part of this story is that we didn't actually know that Pumpkin was pregnant. We had taken her in for a checkup at the local vet. There was something hanging out of her behind. At first the vet said it was a penis, but recanted and declared that it was a piece of fur and pulled it out. As it turned out, she was actually giving birth, and the vet had pulled off part of the newborn's tail. The kitty turned out fine, and a good friend adopted him and called him Short Stuff.

Freckles

Freckles was a purebred German Shorthair Pointer. Freckles, Freckie as she later came to be called was from the local shelter. I remember the day we went out to look. It was my first time at the shelter. I must say it was quite a shock. I wasn't prepared for what I saw I wasn't looking for any particular dog and there are so many dogs. I went with my friend, Nancy, and we spent some time looking around. We stopped at one particular cage and there was a beautiful dog looking up at us with very sad eyes. I asked an attendant to open the cage so we could get a better look and go for a walk. All of a sudden she burst out of the cage and jumped into my arms. I looked surprisingly at Nancy and she said, "I guess you found the right one". It was at that point that I realized that no matter how much thought and preparation you put into finding the right dog, it's not your decision. They choose you!

It was apparent after a few weeks that Freckie had been trained as a hunting dog. When we would take her for walks it would take forever. She would go on point for every--squirrel, bird, and cat in the neighborhood. Not knowing the command to stop her, it took some time to allow her to learn to relax.

Freckie lived with Sheva for a few years and they became great buddies.

I loved her dearly, but Freckie had one personality quirk. She was terrified of thunderstorms. Whenever a storm was approaching, she would instinctively know hours ahead of time. She would start to pace and pant. The closer the storm, the more intense her fretting. When the thunder would start, especially at night, she would curl up around my head and shake until it was over. Oddly enough, she would stop as soon as the storm had passed. Somehow she knew the danger was over.

I've never understood how animals get the same diseases as humans but Freckie got cancer. It was in it's early stages when it was diagnosed so I had some time to prepare myself for the day when she would not be around. Through the process I took her frequently to be examined by the vet. As a result, I met a very compassionate person. It turned out, after becoming a vet he found out that he was allergic to animal dander, but he continued to practice because of his commitment to the animals. He kept telling me that I would know "when it was time". I did not want Freckles to be in pain, but I also struggled with making a decision too quickly. I prayed that she would pass in the night, but that was not to be God's will. One morning when I let her out, I stood sadly by the door watching her. I knew it was time. I called Nancy and we took her to the vet's office. We stayed with her and comforted her. As painful as it was, and continues to be, I feel that I owe Freckles that much for all the love that she gave me. Freckie was around 14 years old when she finally passed; she was a good friend and she is missed greatly.

The Farm

After a year or so of looking Nancy purchased a beautiful farm. It is sixteen acres of rolling countryside and a very relaxing place to be. It's quiet with a lot of birds and animals just having fun. In addition to the pasture for the horses there are also two large hay fields. It wasn't long before we became urban cowboys. Nancy purchased a tractor, mower, and hay bailer. Never having cut and bailed hay before I called upon the expertise of my son, Christopher, whom has worked on a farm since his early teens. He told me how to drive the tractor and what pitfalls to lookout for. So off we went cutting down the hay. It was a lot of fun once you got the hang of driving the tractor--a piece of cake. Then we changed pieces of equipment and raked the hay into rows. Now came the interesting part attaching the hay bailer. Once we figured out how to set everything on the bailer, the machine did all the work. We ended up with around 400 bales of hay, which was more than enough for the two horses. The hardest part was picking up all the bales in the field and stacking them in the barn.

So now we were officially farmers. Now if you're a farmer reading this you can stop rolling your eyes. None the less, it was fun, tiring fun and definitely a rewarding and a learning experience.

The farm was soon to become, little did we realize at this time, a refuge for rescued animals.

The Horses

Jasper

Nancy and I have two very close friends and they had racehorses. We have a horseracing track in our town and on occasion we would go with our friends for an evening out. Their horse named "A Touch of Style" was a very beautiful pacer and they were very proud of her and her track accomplishments. During several conversations with them we had discussed going into partnership with them and a few other horse people. It is quite expensive to own and train a racehorse and the idea of a partnership was to lessen the costs to everyone. It sounded like a fun investment so we proceeded and eventually we purchased a three-year-old horse named Blue Creek Jasper. Jasper is a beautiful horse standing around 16.5 hands high. Equines are measured in hands. One hand is equal to four inches so Jasper would have been 66 inches at the shoulders commonly known as the whithers. He had shown great promise as a two year old and had turned in some very fast times. Everyone was excited about our new acquisition. Our trainer who was also one of the partners noticed that he seemed to be having some problems with his footing. He tried several horseshoes and nothing seemed to be working.

Puzzled, he asked the track veterinarian to watch him go around the track. It only took two laps for the vet to make his diagnosis. It seems that Jasper has what is known as protozoan myelitius. It affects how the signal from the brain reaches the legs and feet. Jasper was a danger to himself and other horses on the track. His racing days were over. A meeting was held on what was to be done about him. The consensus was to cut the groups losses. This can be achieved by several means. One was to put the horse down or two is to sell him to the Amish and let them work him in a field until his time is up. This was all very foreign to Nancy and me and not being professional horse people seemed quite harsh. At one point in the meeting I spoke up and asked if he was left alone in a pasture would he be OK. The answer was somewhat a puzzling yes. So, Jasper could go out in the field and just be a horse? The answer came back yes but why would you want to do that.

I think it was at this point looking back is where I started to become a true animal lover. Oh, yes the group said if we wanted him that we could have him. Nancy and I immediately started to look for a pasture where we could put Jasper. I'll never forget the day when we let him out. He got off the trailer, held up his head flared his nostrils and took off running through the field. He was out in the field for a couple of months but he was not getting the attention that he needed and some of the stronger horses were beating up on him. Nancy found an apartment on a farm with a stall and pastures in which Jasper could stay. After Nancy moved we borrowed a horse trailer and moved Jasper to his new home. This was a much better environment for him and we could give him the attention and care that he needed. We would work with him regularly; lunging him daily (walking and pacing him on a 20 ft. lead rope in a circle) and making him walk between logs and obstacles.

We were not going to give up on him. We both felt that if we continued to work with him that he could be a "normal" horse again. We made arrangements to take him to Ohio State University of Veterinary Medicine. There we met Dr. Reed, one of the top neurological veterinarians in the country. After examining Jasper he came up with the same conclusion as everyone else. Though he did say if we worked with him he could improve some. He got to the point where he seemed to lose almost complete control of his limbs. There is a veterinarian who practices holistic medicine on animals. I always referred to him as Dr. Voodoo; his real name is Dr. Hawthorne. Jasper could never turn his head or neck to the right and Doc. Voodoo was using acupuncture and chiropractic on him. One day after a treatment the Doc started pinching his belly like a fly was biting him. To our shock and amazement Jasper turned his neck around to the right and bit his belly. We continued to work with Jasper until he was able to go out in the pasture with the other horses and be their equal. I had a video camera and Nancy wanted to take a video of Jasper running in the field and send it to Dr. Reed. It was a pretty neat video because we dubbed in the music Raindrops Keep Falling on my Head. Now over eighteen years later, when I see Jasper running in the field or just standing majestically so proud, that song comes to mind and I shed a little tear.

Ozzie

I had grown increasingly disenchanted with the horseracing business. I was having problems with the treatment of some of the animals. There are many good and caring trainers and owners but there is the "win at any cost mentality" that I object to. Nancy continued on as an owner when she purchased another horse. His name was Osborne Starwave. He was roan in color(sort of strawberry blonde) with a beautiful blonde mane and tail. Ozzie had been racing for several years and had his share of wins, places, and shows (first seconds and thirds). He had a problem when he was racing that he would knock his front knee and it would get pretty torn up at the end of the race. But Ozzie was a true competitor and athlete. No matter what, Ozzie would always jump out in front of the crowd and at least for the first half mile he would be in the lead. Towards the end of his career you could still expect the same performance from him but his knee wouldn't hold up and Ozzie usually ended up in last place but still running like he was in the lead. When it became obvious that he couldn't race anymore Nancy brought him back to the pasture so he could be with Jasper and the other horses. Of course the first thing he did was to jump the fence into the neighboring farm. When first brought into a pasture most racehorses are still high strung but it didn't take long for them to realize that they wouldn't be training and racing anymore.

When Nancy bought her farm Ozzie came along with Jasper. After she moved in and got settled. We fenced in about six acres and brought Ozzie and Jasper to their new home. It was really nice to see them together "just being horses". It's been over twelve years since Nancy purchased the farm. Last year Ozzie suddenly became sick, and soon after he passed away. It was one of the saddest days of my life and until this day I've never gotten over his passing. Of the many things I will always remember about Ozzie and I feel that it is his most endearing quality was his quivering lip. It meant nothing except it was a twitch. You would look at him and his lower lip would quiver. As it always did and is doing now it's bringing a smile to my face. Ozzie died in Nancy's arms as he lay in his stall. We had him buried in the opposite field. It happened to be the same field that during the first week that Nancy had moved to the farm it rained that day and soon after the rain had stopped a small rainbow appeared in that very field. I have no idea if there was any meaning attached to that except that as it turned out it happened to be the final resting-place for many animals that we have loved over the years.

I would like to share a poem that I wrote soon after Ozzie's death.

Your strength and ability was something to behold
Your willingness to succeed was unmatched
Your pride was unparalleled

27

Although your success was not always forthcoming
Your desire to never give up is something that I'll always
remember
It is that desire that I sometimes reach back for
If that is your legacy then everyone should have known you
For those who have, you have touched
Run my friend, run free and fast

As I am writing this book it came to me that there needed more to be said about Ozzie. As you have gathered there was a very special bond between the Oz man and me. I would just love to go lean on the fence and watch him. Now you're going think I've really gone mad. After Ozzie died I would go over to his gravesite and just sit and talk to him. It really made me feel good for one thing and I've just not gotten over his death. Several times I would just lay down in the field next to him and close my eyes. I could actually envision him standing over me. I could feel his presence and then there he would be standing over me. This would last for awhile and then I could tell he was gone.

Recently I had to have some very serious surgery. The night before the surgery I was lying in my hospital room trying to get some sleep and I got a vision of Ozzie in my mind. He was standing in the middle of the pasture with a beam of light shining down on him. He looked beautiful and regal at the same time. I don't know exactly how long the vision lasted but when it was gone I tried my best to get it back but to no avail. I felt a calm come over me and I knew that whatever the result of the operation I was going to be fine. I finally went to sleep and except for Nancy I haven't told anyone else until now.

Oz will always be with me and that's just fine

As it turned out not only was the farm a fun place and a new home for the horses it also became somewhat a refuge for many rescues in the years to follow. In all actuality our first rescue predated the farm by one year, but it's my book so you'll have to play along.

Luke

Luke is a miniature donkey. You've probably seen them at petting zoos. If not well they are just the cutest animals. He probably stands about three feet high and weighs about a hundred or so pounds. After Ozzie had passed away we were worried about Jasper. There is a so-called urban legend that you can't leave a horse in a pasture without his pasture mate or they will die of loneliness. I have no idea how much truth there is to that rumor but it certainly plays on your mind and we didn't want to take the chance. Several people had suggested that we get a goat and one suggestion was a donkey. We had heard about a local farmer that raised miniature donkeys so we went out to investigate. Shortly after arriving at the farm we got our first glance of a miniature donkey. He was only eight months old and absolutely adorable. We talked with the breeder for a good while asking as many questions as possible. We thanked him for his time and drove off. Driving back home we decided to stop at Starbucks and get some coffee. While we were enjoying our cup of joe, we discussed the donkey and decided that we just had to get one.

So back to the farm we drove and after walking around the pasture for a while we picked out the donkey we wanted or, as I like to say he picked us. Now the problem how to transport him back home. A horse trailer was out of the question; he would have gotten lost in it. I own a Toyota pickup with an access cab. We moved the front seat forward and folded up the back seat and lined it with a tarp from the bed. I picked him up; he only weighed seventy-five pounds and put him in the back seat. So off we drove with a donkey in the cab of the truck. Only once on the rideback did we encounter a surprised look from an oncoming driver. She probably is still in therapy today! After arriving home and taking him out of the truck we introduced him to Jasper. If a horse could have a puzzled look on his face, Jasper did. He simply didn't know what to make of him. As a comparison Jasper is sixteen and a half hands high, while Luke is only around four. Jasper weighs approximately twelve hundred pounds and Luke now weighs around one hundred and twenty,

It didn't take long for them to become buddies and Jasper has become very protective of his little friend. It's funny seeing them running in the field. Jasper has a long graceful stride and Luke is trying to keep up with a short choppy gallop. There is a biblical story about donkeys. It seems that when Christ was on the cross there was a donkey near by. The image of the cross-appeared on his back and since that time certain donkeys are born with an image that appears to be a cross, down their back and across their shoulders. Hearing that story we felt that we were blessed and Nancy named him Luke from the book of Luke in the Bible.

The X-File Dogs

Kodi
The first X-File dog

I live in an older neighborhood near a major interstate. It's
not often but not uncommon to find strays from time to
time. One fall day in 1992 I don't remember the exact date
but it was the day of the first episode of the Xfile television
program. I looked out the living room window and saw a
little black puppy running around in the neighbor's yard. My
mother who lived with me at the time said it didn't belong to
anyone it just came around the other day and the neighbors
were feeding him. I walked across the street and asked what
they planned to do with him. He was really cute. He was all
black and fuzzy like a little bear cub. Hence, his name Kodiak
which was shortened to Kodi. The neighbors didn't want him
and said if I wanted him to take him. After grabbing him
up I jumped into my car and took him straight to Nancy's
apartment. She happened to be out in the stables with Jasper
and I walked in with Kodi and that was it love at first sight at
least that the way is was with Nancy and Kodi. There is so
much to be said about Kodi and I'll try my best to give you the

best readers digest version that I can. From the very first he was the best and smartest dog I've ever encountered. He loved to go for rides and play in the fields. He had one bad habit and that was to bark and chase after the horses. We believe that he got kicked one time because he's had trouble with his jaw for years. There was a dump over on the other side of the hill at the farm and Kodi would go to the dump everyday and play. What exactly attracted him to that area we don't know but he sure loved to go there. That is where he earned his alternate name of Stinky. He would come back from the dump and smell. He was always getting a bath. To this day we still call him Stinky. Kodi would be the closest thing to a child that Nancy and I would have. If that gives you any inkling of how much he meant to us. Nancy has always lived by herself and for all these years I know that she looks forward everyday to coming home to find Kodi waiting for her at the door.

I know everyone reading this will say that his or her dog is the smartest. And I'm sure that you're right. When Kodi was a pup he had a toy box filled with his favorite toys. It was cute to watch him he would go over to the toy box and pick through the toys to find the one he to play with at the time. He could open his Christmas gifts better than most people I know. We would always give him his gifts wrapped in paper and tied with a bow. Kodi would carefully untie the bow and then unwrap the gift, most times without damaging the paper. During his first winter with us we found a box and took him to the nearest hill and let him sled ride, he loved it. Jethro whom you don't know yet would get loose on occasion. The first time he ran off I was in the barn working and I didn't know what to do. Kodi had been inside so I brought him out and explained that Jethro was missing and he needed to bring him home. Kodi turned and ran under the fence and started trotting across the pasture and into the woods. Not fifteen minutes later I heard a bark and turned to see Kodi standing with Jethro. That was thirteen years ago and although he moves around a little slower now I look into his eyes and still see that little puppy running around the barn.

Licorice
The Other X-File dog

T hree years had passed and another strange occurrence happened. The whole incident was out of the ordinary. Nancy had come over to my house so we could walk around the neighborhood. That in itself was an out of the ordinary occurance Nancy very rarely came to my house. As we were walking and talking we noticed a little black puppy come running off a porch and into the street to greet us. She was adorable, very young probably eight to ten weeks old. We picked her up and played with her for a couple minutes and then took her back to the porch and told her to stay. We continued to walk and were laughing about the cute little pup. I never gave her another thought except when I came home from work the next day my son told me to go look in the basement. When I got to the bottom of the steps I got the shock of my life. It was the little black puppy. She ran over to me and we played for a few minutes. My son informed me that when he got home she was just sitting in the front yard.

I told him about our encounter last night and we gathered her up and drove down to the house from where I saw her last. I knocked on the door and rang the doorbell but no one was home. The person in the next house informed me that the house had been vacant for several months and the little puppy had just appeared about a week ago and as far as he knew didn't belong to anyone. This house is over a quartermile from my place and not visible at all. I thought it was really strange that the little pup came to my place. Later that night I called Nancy and informed her about the find. It was then that she reminded me the night we walked around the neighborhood that once again it was the season premier of the Xfiles.

I named her Licorice because as it turned out she appears to be a mix between a Cocker Spaniel and Chow. She has a black tongue and it looks like she has been eating black licorice. She also went out to the farm and Kodi and her have been buddies for ten years now. Licorice has developed a bladder problem so we put in a dog door that leads out into the backyard. She just loves it now she can go outside anytime she wants.

Mama Dog

Mama Dog

I suppose it's time to tell you about Mama Dog. I was getting ready for work one morning. I live in a quiet neighborhood one I'm quite familiar with. I grew up there and after fifteen years or so eventually moved back and purchased my parent's home. Three doors down lived an elderly woman whom had lived in the same house for the past forty years. As I was coming down the front steps I happened to see her out in the front of her house and something seemed to be wrong. I put down my case and walked over to her to see if I could help her out in any way. She was frantic. It so happened that a mother dog had taken up residence under her garden shed. She said there were puppies but not sure how many. She had called the township office and they were sending over someone to get rid of the dog. As I was standing there talking to her two of the three stooges drove up in the township vehicle, It was apparent they had no idea how to help the lady with her problem. These guys were so useless that when the dog barked at them they both ran up on the porch.

I went home to get some food and thought I could coax her out. She had implanted herself under the shed obviously to protect her pups. Well my plan started to work. I would throw her some food and she would come out and then run back under the shed. So I told Moe and Curly that I would try to get her to come out completely and they could net her. She cautiously would come out further and further each time. To the point that she would be almost ten feet or so from the shed. She crept closer and closer towards us and had they waited a couple of seconds longer we would have caught her. Instead we scared her off so I went back home and got my son to come over and help. He crawled under the shed and said, "There are a lot of puppies under here".

I got a laundry basket and he started handing them out. We were up to seven and he said he thought there were only three more. He was correct we ended up with ten puppies probably about a week old. Moe and Curly were dumb founded. I explained that I would take responsibility for the puppies and they could go back to work. They were the cutest guys, not Moe and Curly the puppies. As it turned out they were border collies. Back home first thing I did was call Nancy and then called off work. Nancy's sister worked for a veterinarian and she advised us on what we needed to get to keep the little guys alive. The first couple of days we bottle-fed them almost hourly all the while looking for the mother. I was leaving food out in the driveway. She was eating it but very elusive never being seen. We would drive around the neighborhood and see her in backyards going through garbage looking for food. After a couple of days we ran an ad in the paper. That day we got a phone call from a lady on the next street over. She explained that the dog would follow her daughter home everyday from school after she got off the bus.

I explained our dilemma and she said she could get the dog into her house and call us. The very next day around three o'clock in the afternoon the phone rang and it was her. I drove to her house and went in with a leash and got the mother dog to come over to me. I put the leash on her and got her into the car. I drove home and took her out and into the basement. We were very nervous it had been almost a week since she ran off and we weren't sure if she would accept her babies. She went over to the box and counted each of them. She looked up at me laid down in the box and her babies started to feed from her. She was a good mother and we were so relieved that we had found her. And those babies were as happy and as hungry as could be. This was the first experience that anyone of us had with newborn puppies. It was interesting to watch nature take care of itself. After a few days we moved the whole crew out to Nancy's farm. It seemed the more likely place for the simple reason that there was more space. Of course we were talking with everyone about what to do with these little guys. A close friend of ours was involved with the local humane society. So we met with them and it was agreed that any homes that we found for the puppies were to be registered through the humane society. This ensured that the people were in the computer system and most important the puppies would have to be spayed or neutered under their guidelines. It also gave the humane society some much-needed money since they operate only on donations, adoptions, and fund-raisers. It didn't take long after the puppies were available for adoption to find homes. After four weeks the puppies are separated from their mother and I often wonder what goes through the mind of animals when that separation takes place.

We were very picky on who we let adopt the puppies although no matter how much you try you never know what the end result will be. The only way I could deal with that was that it was the perfect match, otherwise I would never let any be adopted. We kept up with as many as we could but over the years we lost touch with everyone except for one. That puppy we named Casey and she is still out at Nancy's as a part of her family. That brings us to the mother. She was such a good mother and dog and so pretty I couldn't put her up for adoption so I kept her and from the beginning we called her Mama Dog.

The Humane Society

The Humane Society

In our original meetings with the shelter we discovered that they had no means of helping pregnant mothers at the facility. They would occasionally find a foster home and on rare occasions, when they would get a pregnant mother she would have to be put down. Many of the pups born at the shelter didn't make it becuase the mother would often reject them. Possibly due to the many other animals there and the many people parading through daily. The shelter at the time was not a no-kill shelter Many of the animals that were too old or not adoptable after a period of time were put down. As a sidebar to the book I have very mixed feelings about no kill shelters. I can certainly understand the humane idea of its existence but on the other hand it has many negative repercussions. I'll talk about this later in the book but for now I just wanted you to know that I have reservations on this matter.

After some lengthy discussions with the staff and talking seriously about the matter amongst ourselves we had made the decision to possibly take in some pregnant mothers out at the farm. Our only experience so far was with Mama Dog and her pups were already born. We were embarking on the entire whelping process from delivery to adoption. Whelping is a term used to describe the delivery process of pregnant dogs. So off we went to prepare the farm for our new endeavor. The garage area at Nancy's is quite large. The previous owner had used it as a workshop so space was not going to be a problem. We moved things around and purchased a ten by ten-foot dog kennel. Looked as if this would work, however fall was already here and winter was soon upon us and the garage wasn't heated. The basement of house had been converted into an apartment for the previous owner's son, so we decided that we would convert that into a whelping area for the mothers.

The time was soon upon us and the shelter called and asked if we would be able to foster our first pregnant female. We agreed and went out to pick her up. She had beautiful long white hair with tan and brown mixed in. Her name was Abbey and she was really pregnant. We were told she could go at any day. At first she was a little apprehensive around me and as it turned the vast majority of dogs at the shelter seemed to shy away from men until they could trust them. Which leads me to believe that much of the abuse of animals that takes place may be at the hands of men.

Robin was our mentor in the whelping process. She had worked at the shelter for several years and was very familiar with the birthing process. We really put her to the test we asked her many questions on what to do and expect. We even had her home phone number with instructions to call at anytime for any reason. It wasn't forty-eight hours later that Abbey seemed to be going into labor. Now I have to add and I'm not sure what God's purpose for this is but this also holds true for human babies they all seem to be born in the middle of the night. I digressed but on with the story. It was around eleven in the evening and my phone rang. It was Nancy frantic somewhat explaining that labor had started. My first response was did you call Robin? I got dressed and went right over. You have to understand that Robin had explained to us what to do when a puppy comes out of the mother. It seems very strange but you grab the puppy firmly in your hands and with some light force draw it up and down between your legs several times until it starts to breathe. This is somewhat like spanking a baby's bottom to get it to cry. See my problem is what happens out in the woods?

As you might have guessed Robin wasn't at home. Yikes! Abbey was into some heavy contractions and soon this blob popped out. We looked at each other and for some reason I guess it was my responsibility to swing the puppy between my legs. I did this several times not knowing how much force or how many times this should happen. I put the puppy down beside its mother and it wasn't moving, nothing happened at all. Then all of a sudden it took a breath and Abbey starting licking it and it found its way to one of her teats. It was as if we had just had our own child. We both started crying. It was truly one of the most amazing moments of my life.

Abbey ended up having seven puppies and all were healthy. I can only imagine what Abbey must have been going through becuase I was exhausted. It was very early in the morning but worth every minute. Abbey was with us for eight weeks. The process is one that after the original birthing the mother takes care of almost everything for the first four weeks. All we do is put down clean papers in the cage and make sure she has food and water. After the fourth week is when we start to work.

The puppies are separated from their mother and we have to start feeding them and cleaning their cage. Well let me tell you that is a chore. Seven puppies sure make a mess and they eat and drink continually. The older they get the more they want out of the cage and the minute you open the door to the cage they all come running out and go flying everywhere. After several trips to the vets' office for checkups and shots it came time to take them back to the shelter for adoption. This is the hardest thing we have to do in the whelping process.

We loaded up the car with the puppies and Abbey and off we drove to the shelter. It only took a couple of days for the puppies to find homes but the mothers are the ones that can take a long time. One of there arrangements we had with the shelter was that under no circumstances would they put down the mothers no matter how long it took for them to get adopted. The hardest part of that day was taking Abbey to the cage shutting the door and saying goodbye to her.

We worked with the humane society for around three years whelping mothers. There was a time when we had three mothers and 24 puppies. Let me tell you when the fourth week came upon us it was unbelievable. There were puppies everywhere. But once again worth every minute. Of course not all the times were happy ones. Sometimes a puppy wouldn't make it. Funny, if you have a dog for years or for only in some cases a couple of minutes, it still hurts just as much. There is nothing like having a newborn puppy in your hand, it's warm and fuzzy it's little eyes closed and that feeling is just something you have to experience. On the other hand when one dies while you're holding it well again it's just something you have to experience

The Dogs

Maxwell

Maxwell what else is there to say? He's a big boy part Irish Wolfhound and part Old English Sheepdog. The best way to describe his appearance is to go to the Dennis the Menace cartoons and take a look at his dog. I give you The Maxwell. Max was one of the original rescues. He was going to be put down and Nancy and I brought him out to the farm with intentions of finding a home for him. Nancy and I put on a Halloween party for her coworkers and friends for several years. It was lots of fun and surprisingly many people looked forward to it. Many of the children would ask their mothers if we were having the party. At one of the parties Max was there and a woman and her daughter were toying with the idea of adopting him. I'm not sure why but I didn't feel comfortable with them as his owners. I couldn't put my finger on it but I put up a roadblock. I decided to adopt him myself.

Maxwell is probably around twelve or thirteen years old. He was supposed to be three when he was adopted. Max has a few silly quirks so I would often call him Silly Dog. He sleeps a lot and doesn't like to be disturbed. He has certain places he likes to be and if he can't be there he will let you know it. He doesn't like thunderstorms but if you cover him with a blanket he'll be OK. He loves to lie next to you in bed. He's very good about it. He will wait until you are in bed and comfortable, then he plops next to you and then gives you one good shove then he's off to sleep for the night. Now as he has gotten older he can't get up on the bed he's tried but can't so he just sleeps on the floor now.

One of if not his most endearing qualities is what I call "countertopping". That simply means if he can reach it on the countertop, he will eat it. My mother god bless her, she is now in a home but for a number of years she lived with me. She has Parkinson's disease. So it was very difficult for her to get around though somehow she managed as long as she could. Faithfully everyday she would make herself a sandwich for lunch. It was quite an operation, some would say it was an ordeal. Never the less she would make her sandwich and put in on the table and then go back into the kitchen and get her milk. On more than one occasion she would return to an empty plate. It was funny because for a moment you could see her thinking to herself did I forget to make the sandwich. Then she would figure out it was Maxwell.

He's actually lying here next to me now as I write about him. He's so furry he looks like a throw rug. His face is next to the furnace register, he loves to have something blowing in his face, hot or cold doesn't matter to Max. These guys are such a part of the family, so much a part of the fabric of my life. I only wish that everyone felt this way, the feeling I have right now is beyond anything I can explain. Why can't this feeling continue, why must it be interrupted? Damn immortality!

Hobo

One Sunday afternoon in August of 2002 my son and I were driving down to the marina to go out on our boat. About half way there an approaching car was flashing its headlights. I thought it was the international sign that a police car was up ahead checking for speeders. Much to my surprise as we crested the hill a little dog was running in the middle of Route 40. I stopped my truck and put on my flashers and honked the horn. The little guy turned around and when my son opened the door, he jumped in.

First thing we noticed was the smell! He stunk awful. His hair was terribly matted and the biggest fleas I had ever seen were crawling all over him. And did I mention the stink? He looked somewhat like a Pomeranian. We continued on our journey to the marina. We had decided just to check on the boat and not stay now that we had an added visitor. As soon as we got down on the docks the little dog jumped into the river. On top of everything else I had a soaked dog. I did mention the stink, didn't I? After drying him off we started home all the while trying to figure out what to do with him. He was not wearing a collar so it was going to be difficult trying to find his owner.

As soon as we got back home I took him to the back yard and got some flea shampoo and went to work scrubbing him. He was matted something terrible and I managed to get some of the worst ones cut out. He seemed to enjoy his bath and afterwards I got him some water and food. He was a hungry little fella, ate all of his food and drank some water. I brought out Mama Dog and Maxwell, one at a time to introduce them to him. They seemed to get along swimmingly, it was kismet.

The next day I made an appointment with the groomer and the vet to have him checked. After his visit to the groomer, he looked adorable. She had to shave him down completely except she was able to give him a little mane around his head. And that stink I kept referring to it had been replaced with a fresh clean smell. Hew, what a relief. His visit to the vets was a little different story. The vet put his age at around 10 years or so. And she said he had been out on his own for quite some time apparently his nutrition was so bad that he had to have several teeth pulled because of it. He also has this really bad cough but it turns out that Pomeranians can have a soft esophagus and they can't take in the proper air, which causes them to have a gag, reflex.

Soon after his adjustment to his new surroundings we had to name him. Because of his background and his appearance when we found him, Nancy suggested Hobo. It fit him perfectly little Hobo was the newest member of the family. Time had come for the annual Halloween pet costume contest sponsored by the area humane society. We decided to enter Hobo and we made his costume you guessed it a hobo complete with a handkerchief pouch on a stick and he also was pulling a boxcar we had made. Hobo won third place and it was a lot of fun.

Hobo has been with me for over three years now. What a great little guy. Recently he's had some health problems and some more teeth had to be removed but he's so cute and has the funniest little things he does that makes coming home that much better everyday. One other thing I almost forgot to mention is when Hobo gets mad or upset at something his bark sounds just like ARF. When you see the words "ARF, ARF, ARF" in a cartoon you now know what Hobo sounds like.

Just recently Hobo wasn't eating and didn't seem his usual self. I made an appointment at the vets and they seemed concerned so wanted to keep him for a while and take some tests. X-rays revealed that he had a growth on his stomach and on his liver and the blood tests said he was in early stages of kidney failure. Of course the vet wanted to do more testing and put him on fluid therapy. We were devastated and in shock but the tests seemed conclusive. The doctor said the best case scenario with therapy would be six months. I told him I had to go home and devour what I had just been told. Nancy went with me of course. She is the brains of this outfit. After talking it over with her we decided not to put him through anymore testing and therapy and to let him be in God's hands.

I finally got him to eat rice and ground meat and I added some natural supplements to his diet. It has been a month exactly today and Hobo seems to be back to his normal self. He eats regularly, plays and jumps in my lap for loving. Do I think he is cured, I would like to believe that but in actuality he probably is in some sort of remission. But the reality is he is happy not being stuck with needles and will live out his remaining days in peace.

Roger

There is a very small town in eastern Ohio called Rogers. Every Friday except in winter they have a flea market. This is some flea market. It must rank as one of the largest in the country. Nancy is quite the auction and flea market person, me not so much. When she could she would get away and go to Rogers. One day in addition to the many items she would acquire there was a special item that she purchased. It was a boxer puppy. He was adorable cropped tail and floppy ears. He was fawn with a white blaze on his nose and chest. There were some people selling their boxer puppies for five dollars each. There were only two of them a roan and a brindle. Not sure why she didn't buy both of them but it was Roger that was the name he was given seeing he came from Rogers it just seemed to fit. Anyway I'll defer back to the love at first sight theory I have. Roger came home in Nancy's father's lap.

Roger in a way had his own business for a while. Nancy and I started a food concession business selling hot sausage sandwiches and french fries at fairs and festivals. During our testing period before we launched the business, the dogs made out like bandits they would get all the left over hot dogs and hamburgers. It just seemed appropriate to name the business after one of the dogs and so it became Roger's Lunch Box. We had hats, tee shirts, and banners made up advertising the business. It was funny people would come up to the trailer and ask if the owner or Roger was around. We would answer no he's not here today. We often thought of hanging up a picture of Roger in the trailer but we just never got around to doing that.

Roger has been with us for eight years now and he is just as cute and playful as he was on the first day Nancy brought him home.

Casey

S weet Casey, she is one of Mama Dog's babies. We found homes for all Mama's babies but she came back to us early on. During the adoption process a mother and young girl came to the shelter and wanted to adopt her. Both Nancy and I were hesitant about this adoption, not sure how you know but you just know. Anyway they met all the criteria of the shelter so they were allowed to adopt her. I believe they gave her the name Casey but there have been so many sometimes it's hard to keep track of it all. In any event it wasn't long before they were calling to bring her back. This happens so many times in adoptions. People fall in love with puppies and don't realize what the breed is and how it acts or they don't realize what is involved with raising and keeping an animal. Ideally the shelters should be educating people on proper care and what a breed demands but they are so overwhelmed and over populated that they tend to overlook these important details. With all the animals we have been involved with in adoptions you just have to close your eyes and hope and pray that they are going to the best home. Casey and Roger are best friends and live and play together. Casey is the same age as Roger an eight-year-old. After Casey came back to us we really didn't try very hard to find a home for her although it would have been the best thing. I suppose there was something about her being Mama's baby that kept her around this long. And to answer your burning question. No Casey and Mama don't see each other. Mama lives with me and Casey of course with Nancy. But I tell Mama everytime I see Casey that I saw her baby and I really believe she knows what I'm talking about.

We have lost touch with all the rest of Mama's babies. We tried for the longest time but it was an impossible task. Bailey was bounced around for a while, one other ended up in the hands of a drug dealer. One though went to a local car salesman and on occasion we would see him and I know that he is being taken well care of.

Jethro

Jethro, dope on a rope may sound a little harsh but then you would have to have known Jethro. Jethro was a bloodhound. A very good friend of mine who also is involved in animal rescue and has been for years introduced me to Jethro. He was going to be put down so she and her husband rescued him from the shelter. He was a big boy weighing over 120 pounds. When I first saw him he was nameless. Diana just called him dope on a rope. Mostly because he was just a slow moving guy. Jethro was around two or three years old. That's what the shelters seem to tag most animals with, around two years in age. He looked a lot like Sheva so there was an instant attraction to him. Once we got Jethro home and his home was on the farm, we both simply fell in love with him. For the first few weeks we would chain him outside the barn, for the reason the fencing hadn't all been put in place yet. Jethro had tons of energy and keeping him indoors at least at first was not possible he would just bulldoze over everything and everybody. But there wasn't a chain made that would hold him. When he would pick up the scent of a critter he would simply just stretch out the chain and it would break. I remember going back to the hardware store and asking for the largest chain they had. The clerk just looked at me and said "I don't want to meet the animal that breaks this chain, it's the largest we carry." Of course once he would break the chain he was off and so was I. As large as Jethro was he could really run fast. I would go back in the woods and search for hours and find no sign of him. Then on one rescue I was walking along the creek and I spotted a rather large black and tan object lying in the middle of the creek. Yes, of course it was Jethro just lying there cooling off. This is the dog Kodi went tracking and brought back earlier on. Jethro's antics sped up the process of getting the fence completed and Jetty as he became known had his own area to roam. We figured that a little over an acre would satisfy him. Oh yea, and to keep him happy we went out and got a plastic wading pool for him to keep himself cool.

Jethro was such a kind and gentle soul that anyone that came in contact with him just fell in love with him. The local shelter has a pet costume contest every year at Halloween. So we decided to enter Jethro. I'm a little bigger than average and I own a pair of overalls, you know the bib type. We tried them on Jetty and they fit him. His costume consisted of a flannel shirt, the bib overalls, and a straw hat tied onto his head, with some straw coming out of his pockets. Needless to say when I was called up on stage the crowd went wild, laughing and clapping. In the end, Jetty took first place in the competition and when we went up to get his ribbon, he got a standing ovation. Like I said, when you saw him you fell in love with him. It's been a couple of years now since Jethro died. He had a heart problem; it was just too big. We buried him in his yard up in the top corner where he used to sit and watch everything.

I wrote a tribute to him I would like to share. I keep it in a frame along with his picture and his first place ribbon.

You came into my life at first as a remembrance
of something in the past.
But soon your very being identified you as that which you
are.
You brought many smiles over our times of existence.
You brought smiles to all those who you touched.
Your time was in many ways so short.
The memories you leave however will last an eternity.
Your will lives on in me.
Your strength lives on in me.
Your fate was chosen for you.
I will not forget you.
I cannot forget you.
You have changed my life forever.
If I can leave a mark such as yours in my life
it will not have been in vain.
Goodbye old friend and if prayers are to be answered then I
will sit by your side again.

Mama Dog & Spanky

Three kitties

Noodles

ozzie

kodi

Nutty

Licorice

Wally and the bear

The Cats

Frosty a.k.a. Nutty

When Nancy rented an apartment on the farm, of course there were always a lot of cats being born. Not surprisingly she acquired several of these kittens. One of these kittens was Frosty. He was an orange tabby and did a lot of silly things. I would always say to him,"You're a nut". After a while he became known as Nutty. Today, Nutty is fourteen years old. Several years ago Nutty was outside doing whatever cats do outside, and he didn't come home.

A week or so went by and still no Nutty. Then one night around eleven o'clock my phone rang and Nancy was crying and saying Nutty came home but he was hurt. I quickly got dressed and drove over to her place. It was true. Nutty had come home but he was badly hurt. It appeared someone had shot him in the face with buckshot. He wouldn't let us touch him anywhere in those areas. And then we suddenly noticed Nutty was blind. Still to this day we have no idea who did this horrible crime nor do we know where Nutty had gone. But what we do know is that Nutty managed to find his way home blind!

Nutty gets along just fine today. Actually, if you didn't know it, you would never know he couldn't see. He bumps into things but he is never deterred. And you can find Nutty in the oddest places. You can open a closet or a kitchen cabinet and Nutty will be sitting in there. He just gets up and walks out. He is still Nutty. It's just another example of how much we can learn from animals. I'm sure many humans could not adapt to their handicap as well as Nutty did. If you think about it he doesn't even know he is handicapped. I'm sure he's confused (however that is in animals) but their adaptability is just amazing.

Mickey and Minnie

Nancy would have to be referred to as the cat person between the two of us. I have a tendency to lean towards dogs even though I have three cats myself. They are very fascinating creatures. Nancy's affinity towards cats is second-to-none. I guess this story goes back around eight or nine years ago. Nancy is also as tax preparer and one of her clients had two kittens that needed a home. There were so small they fit in your hand and were slate gray making them look like two mice. Hence there names Mickey and Minnie.

After a period of time Minnie became very ill. We took her to the vets and they suggested isolating her until they could determine her illness. We placed her in the bathroom and she had been in there for several days when she took a turn for the worse. We had braced ourselves for the worst. On the other hand her brother Mickey was as healthy as he could be full of energy. Even though Mickey showed no signs of his sisters illness we kept him in the room next to the bathroom isolated also just incase he was carrying the same disease.

We had both gone to work that day. I had arrived at Nancy's house before she had gotten home. I immediately wentpuppies into the bathroom to check on Minnie and got the shock of my life. Somehow Mickey had gotten into the bathroom. To my amazement I found Minnie sitting up and looking as if she had never been sick and Mickey was lying dead at her feet. I grabbed a towel and wrapped Mickey in it and then I picked up Minnie and checked her all over. Amazingly she was fine. I was in total shock and it then hit me what had happened.

You have to understand me; my beliefs are somewhat weird. I"m not a very religious person but I am a very spiritual person. In this instance and still to this day I believe that it was by design that Mickey got into the bathroom and he gave his life, soul and essence to his sister. I called Nancy at work and when she got on the phone I couldn't speak. That is my give away, when she heard my silence she immediately assumed that Minnie had passed away. She never expected to hear what happened.

Minnie continued to grow and seemed to be healthy. Then one-day Nancy noticed she seemed to be having trouble walking around. She looked into her eyes and they seemed a little cloudy. We took her to a specialist in feline vision and he told us what we didn't want to hear. Minnie was going blind. The only thing we could do for her was to take her home and love her. Minnie is still with us and getting along just fine.

Dr. Nabil Damian

S oon after we had started fostering and rescuing animals it became apparent that the vet bills would be astronomical. We had talked with many of the local vets but none of them seemed willing to help monetarily. A friend suggested that we talk with Dr. Nabil Damian. He had a private vet practice in town, in many ways it was a clinic. You didn't make an appointment; he had walk-in morning and evening hours. And his prices were more than reasonable. This enabled many pet owners who could normally not afford to have their animals cared for the opportunity to do so.

Dr. Damian said he would help us out when we needed him, and boy did we ever use him. He treated our animals and us very well, and many times he would just give us the medication or a treatment at no charge. We often called upon him for advice and he would gladly give it. As I am now reminded (like I said we have had so many animals it's hard to remember), during our first birthing experience, it was Dr. Damian that helped us induce Abbey's labor. He said that probably the first baby would be stillborn. Even more reason for our jubilation when the first puppy was born alive!

Dr. Damian and his family were from Egypt. He was born there and after his education moved to the United States. He first worked for the USDA before opening his veterinary practice. Sadly, he was taken too soon from this earth. On a vacation in the Caribbean, he had a heart attack and died while diving in the reefs.

In addition to being a great veterinarian, Dr. Damian was also a good friend. You will be sadly missed, my friend. Thank you.

Duckland

A little over five years ago, the seventh of June, I was over at the farm doing some work in the pasture. It was early afternoon and whatever I was doing required some help. I went inside to ask Nancy for assistance. Only to find out that she was getting dressed to go somewhere with her friend Kathy. And she was being very secretive. I remember being very angry because I really needed some help with my project. So off she went and I angrily went back to the job at hand.

Several hours had passed and I noticed her coming up the driveway. I had finished my work and was taking a break when she got out of the car and proceeded to get a large box out of the back. She struggled with the box, then came over to me and said "Happy Birthday". You see the next day was my birthday. Now I really felt bad. She had gone out to get me a gift (but I was still thinking she could have gotten it anytime). As it turned out, I was wrong. Friday afternoon was the only day she could have gotten it. I know you are wondering what was in the box. So was I because the box was making noise and moving.

I opened the box and it was filled with little ducks! Five white ducks and two mallards, they were all ducklings. Running around and peeping just like you would expect. They were so cool. It has to go on record as one of the neatest if not the neatest gift I've ever gotten. We kept them in the garage until we could set up a little building and fence. The next day we started on a new project, a building complete with an entrance and ramps. We fenced off an area and temporarily bought them a wading pool. To complete the area we needed a name. Years earlier we had owned a card and gift shop. One of the items we had was a six-foot stork, which we rented to parents to announce the birth of their baby. We would place the stork in the front yard and write the date, weight, baby's name etc. It was now clear why we had kept the giant stork. After finishing the area, we put up the stork and dubbed the place Duckland.

After a year or so we noticed eggs in Duckland. After doing some research we found out that if they were fertile it would be possible for the mother duck to hatch a duckling. And that's exactly what happened. It was a pretty exciting time. As the duckling started to get older we noticed that he didn't seem to be feeling well. We contacted a vet and they suggested we isolate him, so armed with a big box and a heat lamp we set off to make him better. Though Nancy is a pharmacist she is also a believer in homeopathic and alternative methods of curing certain ailments. Using her juicer Nancy would make him a carrot juice cocktail and put it his bowl everyday. One day when we were coming into the garage we passed the duckling and noticed he had dribbled carrot juice all over his chest. It looked as if the had been eating spaghetti. From then on he became know as Noodles. He was the only duck we had ever named. Noodles soon got better and we returned him to Duckland to be with the others. Eventually, we dug out a pond for them to play in and soon had to expand the area. We were told the mallards would eventually fly off. Of course we didn't believe them but as it turned they were correct. The mallards were starting to fly off and would be gone for several hours and then one day they didn't return. I can remember them taking off and watching them flying and wondering if this would be the day they wouldn't return. When they didn't return I wasn't sad but happy that they were finally able to be ducks. I only hope that they are safe and raising little ducklings somewhere. Often when I see mallards in a stream or pond close by I wonder if it is them.

We kept Duckland going for over a year since the mallards flew off and I enjoyed watching them. They would quack and waddle around then dive in the pond but we knew that it wasn't fair to them to be kept in such a small confinement. Now we needed to decide what to do with the white ducks. The industrial park where Nancy worked also had office buildings in another part of town, and she found out that there was a large pond with close to a hundred ducks. They were well taken care of and people would come and feed them daily. We made the decision that it would be better for the ducks if we would take them to the pond and release them. After checking out the place, we gathered up Noodles and his clan and transported them over to the pond. They immediately took to the new place like ducks to water. Sorry. It was sad but knowing they would be with the other ducks and watching them swimming in the big pond we knew we had done the right thing. There were many other white ducks there, but when we go to visit we are pretty sure that we can still tell which one is Noodles.

Her Journey

About Her

Nancy is a very difficult person to describe. She's one of those people that you have to get to know to understand. She stems from a middle class family consisting in addition to a mother and father, to two sisters and one brother, of which she is the youngest. By trade she is a pharmacist, and on occasion an entrepreneur. She is very intelligent and expects a lot of people. Meaning that when your are working, she expects you to work. She doesn't understand when someone stands around and chitchats (her term). But on the other hand, when she is not working she likes to have fun. She is quick-witted, very sincere, thoughtful, and most of all, compassionate. She is very giving, fair, and loving. She becomes very passionate in whatever she is doing. And you never know what she will be passionate about next. And I have to admit that no matter how much I resist, her passions become my passions. And as you will come to find out as much as our personalities differ, they are very much the same.

Changes

Animals have a way of changing our lives, and the lives of those around us. My first memories of a pet are of a dog named Rusty. We lived in a rural area and Rusty was allowed to roam. It was the early 1960's and this was acceptable behavior. We didn't have many neighbors and these wern't many other dogs around, but somehow Rusty would manage to get into fights, and would come home covered with blood and battle scars. I can remember my father losing his patience and kicking the dog down into the basement to punish him. I don't remember trips to the vets, so Rusty must have been resilient enough to overcome the pain, and got better on his own. Then he would repeat the behavior and get into another fight. It was a very ugly scene, and would make one believe that my dad was an awful person.

But times change, and so do people...

In the 1970's my sister worked for a veterinarian, and on occasion would rescue dogs that clients brought in as strays. Such was the case with a black wire haired terrier mix. She was quite a specimen--all matted and smelly--but very loving, and she had a "set of those eyes", bright and sparkly. At this point in his life, my dad had retired with many interests. He enjoyed the outdoors, and loved to garden. Since my sister was having some difficulty acclimating "Rags" into her household, she decided to give Rags to my dad. He was reluctant, but soon found that he had a loyal companion. Rags followed him everywhere and watched that nothing happened to him. She sat in the garden as he planted and cultivated, and later as he picked the fruits of his labor. At the day's end she was glued to his hip as he took a nap in his favorite chair. She traveled beside him in his car, as he did errands, and as he visited tax clients. She listened as he spoke to her, now with loving phrases----she was his "sweetheart". Rags grew older and moved slower, and the time came that my dad made the decision to have her euthanized. He stayed with her, and held her. He brought her home and buried her. He didn't cry in front of us, he was much too proud a man, but I know he wanted to. We suggested getting another dog. He wouldn't have any parts of it. The pain was too fresh.

So I decided to try another avenue. I found a small black and white kitten and I gave it to him as a birthday present. The kitten, as all kittens are, was very, very playful. My dad nicknamed him Bad Boy, and the name stuck. He was soon to become my dad's constant friend. As I stated earlier, times change. Throughout the lives of Rags and Bad Boy, my dad was educated concerning the benefits of spaying and neutering, and maintaining the health of his furry friends. He considered them companions, and not merely animals.

In 1994 my dad had a heart valve replaced. As a complication, he had a leg amputated and had to go to a rehab center. The promise was made that in two weeks he could go home, at least for a weekend. The weekend arrived, and he was notified that the visit was not going to happen. The devastation was obvious from the look on his face. I feared that all of his hard work to walk again would be negated. So, I decided to bring "home" to him. I got Bad Boy, concealed him, and took him to the rehab center. This was probably the first case of "pet therapy" in the center, and the staff didn't even know it happened.   My dad's face lit up when Bad Boy came out of hiding. He jumped on the bed, purred, and cuddled with his buddy. Likewise, my dad had the same reaction. He regained momentum, and soon returned HOME to be with his family and cat.

Replacement valves have a life span of ten years, and such was the case with my dad. In those ten years, I watched as he was transformed from the man of my childhood memories (a very hard, uncaring man who kicked animals) into a very sensitive man who was able to express his love for his family. In his last days he was devoted to taking care of Bad Boy. He gave him a special spot on his bed, fed him every morning, and constantly worried when he didn't come home on time. Because of his concern for Bad Boy, and his ability to express that love, he also learned to open up and verbalize his feeling of love for his family.

As I stated earlier, when he had Rags, he reached a point where he knew it was time to let her go. I don't profess to have any control over life and death, but we as humans, also reach such a point where we know that we must acknowledge that "it is time". On a cold January day, my dad was having a "quiet" day. He was sitting in his wheelchair by the window holding Bad Boy. He was lapsing in and out of consciousness, and not being very responsive. I asked him if he remembered his dog Rags, and he acknowledged with a headshake. I said. "Maybe it's times to go and find Rags, and go for a walk". He met her the next day, along with Rusty. I hope they are walking in a garden.

The Adventurer

His name was Frosty, but he became known as Nutty. You would never know where you would find him-on top of a telephone pole, in the sofit and fascia of the garage, hiding in the barn under the bales of hay looking for a mouse, sitting in the roof gutters looking over the edge at the world below.

When I moved to my farm, I allowed the cats the freedom to roam. It was always my rule of thumb that if they went out to explore and didn't return within three days, I would start to worry. If five days went by, the chances were slim that they would return.

It was ten days, and then two weeks. I had all but given up hope. Nutty had gone out, and had not returned. Then, a miracle-- he showed up, crying on the front porch. I was ecstatic! He looked a little weary and hungry, but otherwise OK. After I took him inside I noticed that his eyes were dilated. Panic settled in. Luckily I found a vet, and after examining him, I was told that Nutty had been "shot full of buckshot" and was blind.

Now, the reality of the miracle started to settle in. I don't know how far he had ventured. Whether it was 100 feet or 2 miles, I was amazed that he found his way home. Whether through his sense of smell or some other unexplained sense, he had navigated his way. And as the days continued he amazed me ever further. If anyone other than me entered a room, he would go to the basement. But when I entered, with or without any audible sound, he would come to me. His ability to sense his surroundings was keener than any human being.

Because of the incident, I kept the cats inside for a while, but eventually I gave in and decided to once again let them roam. I have a small fenced area off the patio, which I reinforced with commercial cat fencing to try to keep their area contained. I installed a pet door in the patio door, and waited. And wouldn't you know it, Nutty was the first cat through the exit. He stuck his little nose by the flap and kept on going. Like the Eveready Bunny he kept going and going-through the barricades, through two gates and ended up in the horse pasture. The horse and donkey had him surrounded and he wasn't moving. Once again, I panic But it was okay. It turned out his pelvis was broken, but a few days in isolation healed him. Now life is back to normal. And I'm waiting for the next exploration.

Yes, that's my Nutty, forever the Adventurer.

What's In A Name

There's always that first "spark" when you meet your new pet. The wet kisses, the cuddling, the laughs over the mischievous behavior all lead to the BIG question "What will we name him?" It might be a physical attribute, a silly movement, or a personality trait. And once it has been decided, I believe the bond is created.

There have been so many. The lost black puppy--the one who looked like a bear--he had to be Kodiak. The rain soaked black wavy haired pup, who licked us with her black tongue-- Licorice was to be her name. The prissy orange and white cat who looked as if she was as delicate as could be, but was as large as she could be....Miss Piggy. The Old English sheepdog who decided to read/destroy a dictionary had to be Webster. There was a litter of kittens all named after candy--Godiva, Hershey, Twix, and Snickers. The kitten found on the Fourth of July had to be Sparkle.The one found outside the bank, our Wall Street kitty, Wallace.

We went fishing on a sunny afternoon to a local lake, Dutch Fork. The warmth of the sun, the silence and the solitude made it a perfect day, but the day became complete when we happened upon a small, white, longhaired cat. She was a matted mess, but when groomed, she looked like the "Fancy Feast" cat. She became known as the Duchess of Fork.

Fleas markets are unfortunately a haven for those who wish to rid themselves of puppies. I would frequent a market in Rogers, Ohio known to be one of the largest in our vicinity looking for bargains, but usually I found myself drawn to the pups. I often rescued them, and brought them back to our local shelter where they would undergo a more formal adoptive process (assuring that they would be spayed/neutered). There was the white pup with brown and black spots--our little JellyBean. The boxer mix, whose tail was cropped along with his dew claws. I think they originally passed his siblings off as pure bred, but his ears and nose grew a little too much so he was being offered as free. He became one of my most loyal companions--a very sensitive, gentle dog who took on the namesake of his origin, Roger.

Naming kittens was always fun. The orange one with the white spot under his neck-Twinkie. And of course, there had to be a HoHo to go along with him, the black cat with the white spot under her neck. Bonnie and Clyde, two of the semi feral cats, who were rescued and returned to their location. Their life would have been less than complete if they had been housebound. The two who hid behind the refrigerator had to be Fridge and Freezer. Penske was the fastest on the farm, powered by mice and birds, not gasoline. Bubbles was of course, champagne in color and very laid back.

The little donkey. We struggled for a name until I was told that he had a holy cross on his back. I looked in the Bible and found a colored plate of the Good Samaritan from the Book of Luke. It featured a donkey carrying the load, and thus my "Little Luke" had his name.

I realize the names are a reflection of my personality and how I perceived them. I often wonder what their perception is of me, and what do they call me? Warmest toes to chew. Always late with dinner. Always waking me up from a nap. Best belly to sleep on. Loving Mom. Whatever their thoughts, I love them all!

Apricots

The sound of a dentist's drill, the long Novocain needle, and the sight of the swirling water going down the drain are images that invoke fear in many people. I have never had this phobia. Instead, I have been blessed with one of the best dentists. His work is painless, and he is one of the nicest guys around. Always concerned that he doesn't cause any apprehension.

I have never understood why dentist go to the trouble of asking questions after they have placed the gray rubber tent in your mouth. It is certainly an advancement in that you don't choke on the water, however how do they expect you to talk? My usual visit consists of lying back, closing my eyes, and blinking occasionally.

This was not the case a couple of years ago when Kim, my dentist, announced "Nance, I think I'm going to get a kitten. I have always been a dog person, but I'm ready to try a cat". I looked as if I had placed my finger in an electrical outlet. The eyes were wide open, I started to flail my arms and uttered through the rubber tent "Got cat for you! Got cat for you!"

After the rubber device was removed, I proceeded to tell him that I had the most amazing cat for him, not a kitten, but the nicest cat in my house. The response as always "If it is such a great animal, why do you want to give it away?" Let me make myself clear. I would love to keep the most affectionate, prettiest, and sweetest animals, but the flip side of the coin is how do you find a home for the "Problem animal"? Hence, I have offered the best of the crowd on several occasions.

The cat that I was offering was Kittles. He had shown up in the yard, so I started to feed him in the wood shed. He was beautiful! He had the clearest blue eyes (Siamese, I would guess), and a blue gray tint to his coat with a striped tail. One day I heard Licorice barking. I went out and found Kittles cowering in a corner. In my haste to pick him up, I got bitten. No big deal. It has happened before. I place him in the bathroom to isolate him, and went about my day's activities. When I returned several hours later, I found him in a puddle of urine. He had not moved. Panic set in , as you must know by now, a common reaction for me. So off to the vets we went.

The vet promptly told me that he needed to test the cat for rabies since he was ill. I guessed that would be OK until he told me that it involved decapitating the cat, and sending his brain to Harrisburg. Whoa! Wait a minute. Not my idea of a good solution. So, I called the Board of Health, got a quick lesson in rabies, and found that I could treat the cat with antibiotics, observe him for ten days, and start myself on the dreaded rabies injections. Actually, the injections aren't bad. And of course, the cat ended up being fine and ALIVE.

So after a discussion, Kim decided he would meet Kittles. I took him to his office. Kim sat on the floor and patiently waited while Kittles smelled around, weaved in and out of cubbyholes, and came to rest on his lap. He fell in love with him (which is more than I can say for his wife Marcia). She was not crazy about the idea, but went along.

Kim promptly took his precious new friend to the local pet store and showered him with every imaginable toy, catnip, and cat tower.... You name it, Kittles got it. The only problem was how to fit it all into a Volkswagen bug. They finally succeeded and went home.

As I stated, Kim's wife did not share his excitement about the new family member. Actually, it looked as if it was going to be a battle, and it seemed very unlikely that Kittles would stay. But as I have already stated, animals have a way of changing situations. There is a common phrase in the Egyptian markets, "We will have apricots tomorrow". It is comparable to "The check is in the mail". Not likely, but it does happen. And so, when Marcia finally accepted Kittles(and she now loves him dearly), he was bestowed with a new name Mish Mish---Arabic for apricots.

The Bridgeville Kids

Aside from giving Mish a wonderful home, and me a beautiful smile, Kim started me on one of the most amazing journeys of my life. I went back for my six month checkup and he said, "Nance, when you're out looking for cats, I'd really like a black one".

Shortly thereafter, I was leaving my office in Bridgeville and saw a black and white cat. I always carry a cat kit (like some folks always have a winter blanket and snow kit). I placed down some food, and easily picked up the kitty. Off we went to the dentist's. Kim loved him immensely, but his daughter loved him more, so Max , the cat, went to live with Dex, the daughter. But Kim wouldn't have to wait too long because as I started to look around the office, I discovered a colony of feral cats living by the local motel dumpsters.

I read all that I could about feral colonies. Cats are labeled "feral" if they are not at all socialized, and fear all humans from any distance. The kitties I found would more likely be termed stray, since they hung around the motel. Dumpsters kitties feeding on what they could find, and they were approachable within eight to ten feet.

There are several programs available which advocate TNR...trap, neuter, and return. The goal is to neuter so that the population is controlled, and to return the animals to an environment where they are best suited--back to their colony, or if they can be socialized, to a new home. The process involves trapping, usually with a Have a Heart cage, neutering, and clipping or notching the left ear and returning the cat. The notching of the ear alerts vets that the cat has already been neutered in case they are caught a second time.

So my mission started. Our office sat on the hill above the motel. Nightly, I drove to the motel and offered food. I found six cats about six months old that frequented the dumpster. My first enlightening experience involved my car. As soon as they heard the sound of MY engine, they would appear. On several occasions, I drove a different car and they did not show up. How did they know? Then I saw a mother with three kittens. They were so elusive, but I prevailed, and finally found that they lived under the motel and their access point was a window well type entrance. The mother was very, very untrusting. I would put out the food, and only when I returned to my car would she eat. She would watch, and one by one the kittens would come up out of the hole. No audible sound from her, no visible sign, but she was definitely communicating with them.

I was further amazed when I was leaving the office one evening, and found the cats outside our office door. They traveled up the hill and knew where to come. Somehow, a sense, that we as humans do not experience, enabled them to find ME.

By now, they were beginning to trust a little more, and I was able to coax several into carriers and close the door behind them. Off to the vets for the "fixing". Tippy was the first and all went OK. Twinkie eluded me so I settled for HoHo. I dropped her off and at the last minute noticed her strange left ear (must have been from a fight). If you remember TNR, you must have guessed. When I went to pick her up, the vet informed me that she had already been spayed. YES, it actually works! Someone besides me was also looking out for these guys.

All in all there must have been twelve cats. Several I returned after neutering. Bonnie and Clyde, two of the most elusive kittens were returned. Clyde disappeared after a flood, along with Tippy. As sad as that was, the flood also provided another enlightening event. I had been feeding a black cat that I knew had kittens hidden somewhere. During the flood, I looked out the back window of the office to see Cinderella with four black and white kittens. She instinctively knew to bring them to higher ground to avoid the danger. They frolicked in the days ahead. Played under the air conditioning units on the lower level and came up to the office nightly for food. Eventually I captured the kittens. Since it was fall and the days were getting darker I gave myself some time to capture Cinderella.

They tell you that cats don't get pregnant in the winter. Well, you can't believe everything you hear. One warm January day, I noticed a new cat hanging around with Cinderella. The cat was only there for one night and then disappeared. Now, I was wise enough to know it was a male, and he was there for only one reason, winter or summer. I continued to feed her, and just before two months elapsed, I captured her. Sure enough, a few days later she had five calico babies. She was the best mom. She never left her kittens. She was content to lay and let them feed 24 hours a day. She would purr, coo, and make little BRRRP sounds when she talked to the girls. And they listened. Once again, I knew she was communicating in a way that far exceeded any verbal means that humans have.

It was time for the girls to be adopted, and it was time for another six month checkup. Once again Kim said "Nance, when you're out looking for cats" and once again his wife Marcia said "NO, not another". But you know who won, and the trade off is that Marcia says this is the first time in 35 years that Kim has agreed to vacuum on a regular basis.

Stop Me

As for my journey, I now have many more cats. I love them dearly

However, there is a disease called cat-hoarding syndrome. It involves rescuing to a point where you can no longer give the appropriate care, and you end up doing more harm than good. I often wonder if I am about to cross that line. But then I visit my vet and she assures me that the cats are healthy with glossy coats and well adjusted. I hope to never cross the line, but if I do, I hope that someone has the courage to confront me.

Let's Play

Our society seems to have programmed us to always need someone around to share our good times and our bad times. It is rare to find someone who is content to be alone with his or her thoughts. To make the most of the serenity of a quiet moment.

Not so with the animals. Cats seem happy to curl up in the warmth of the sunshine on a windowsill. They purr until they fall asleep. When they awaken, they exhibit stretches that would be the envy of many yoga instructors.

And when they play, they surely enjoy every second. There is no need for high tech. Give a kitty a windy, autumn day and they can be amused for hours chasing leaves. Chasing snowflakes is certainly more fun than skiing or sledding, unless you would be my dog, Kodi. When he was a youngster he was playing in the backyard on a snowy day. Given that he had a long furry coat, he didn't mind the cold. He found a cardboard box, the old variety used for cases of canned sodas--a 12 by 18 rectangle with a 2 inch lip around the edge. Kodi went about the yard pulling, tossing, and tugging. At one point he was on the hill. He planted his paws firmly inside the box as he tugged back with all his force. WHISH, down the hill he went. WOW, that was fun so he tried it again, and again, and again. Until of course, we got out the video camera. Goodbye to that possible $10,000 video.

Then there was the day that Nutty discovered the birdhouse. Darn those bluebirds. He'd get so close, and then they'd fly into their house on the fence post. Well, he decided to outsmart them. He jumped onto the post, sat on top of the house, and waited. Of course, nothing was coming out so he placed his paw inside the opening. Must have been quite a frightening sight for the feathered guys. Once again, no video.

There were however, times when we were successful with the camera. In his puppy days, Kodi was known to be mischievous when I was at work. So we decided to produce "Home Alone with Kodi". I worked an eight-hour shift with a short drive back and forth so we figured an 8-hour tape would suffice. We set the timer, placed the camera, and off I went to work. Previous untaped episodes included broken barriers, toys on and under every piece of furniture (most of which had been chewed), plants turned upside down with dirt everywhere, and shoes transformed from pumps into sandals. We could only imagine what he was going to do, and what the sequence would be.

After eight hours had elapsed, I was ready to go home. I placed a call and left an audible message on my answering machine to let Kodi know that I was on my way. Yes, I am a little crazy; maybe very crazy. Anyway, with much anticipation I entered the house. It looked as if it had snowed inside-- feathers and down EVEYWHERE. He obviously had a pillow fight, and the pillow lost. If you ever want to play a horrible trick on someone, remember this one. It is next to impossible to vacuum goose down.

And one last postscript--there was no evidence on the video. The tape ran for eight hours, no pillow fight, and no video of Kodi misbehaving. Just a quiet day in the living room. Then just before the tape stopped, we could hear the phone ringing.

Trust

As you know from Bob's story, I own a sixteen-acre farm, and as fate would have it, the space enabled me to become a foster parent through the local animal shelter. I started by bringing home a large, goofy, shaggy dog, Maxwell. Of course, I fell in love with him, and he became a permanent fixture and was adopted by Bob.

So, I decided to try another avenue. The shelter was always looking for "midwives". Many strays come fully loaded, expecting puppies. And the facilities usually are not staffed to accommodate. So Bob and I started our journey as foster parents for the moms and babies.

Our first foster was DeeDee. She came to us from the shelter with three puppies attached, literally. She actually had five pups, but since she delivered during the night and no one was there to assist, she lost two pups. Which is why foster parents are so important. Nature has a way of giving the moms the instinctive nature to birth, clean and feed, but a little help is always welcome. Anyway, back to DeeDee. I called her our "miniature German Shepherd". She was actually some sort of terrier, but she could have been a 15-pound shepherd. She was brown with black saddle pads and the BIGGEST upright ears on any little dog. We always wondered when she would grow into her ears. Bus she was, of course, already full-grown. She was a good mom, and when her puppies were adopted, we decided to keep her for a while. She must have been upset with the added weight of pregnancy, because she quickly set about losing the pounds and toning. She loved to run in the woods, and they must have seemed BIG woods for such a little lady. She would roam for hours, but would return promptly on a whistle. As her final exercise, she would do a leaping jump into our arms. Guess she thought we were in training as tight ends for football season. Then one day we got a call from the shelter that it was National Adoptathon Week, and they wanted DeeDee for the event. It didn't take long for someone to discover our little lady. Her training would come in handy. A cancer survivor who planned on walking daily adopted her.

Abby was our first mom to deliver at my house. Since it was near Christmas our veterinarian had limited hours. We weren't sure when she would go into labor, so he gave us a syringe of pitocin, in case we needed to induce. We knew nothing about delivering puppies, not alone inducing labor, so I was constantly reading books. Abby started to get anxious, she panted, and started to paw at the box, which seemed to indicate labor. But nothing happened. We waited, and still nothing happened. She was exuding a greenish discharge, so I called the vet. He said that the first puppy was probably stuck in the canal, that it was probably dead, and that we needed to induce. OK! No Problem! We took a deep breath, gave her the shot, and waited. It seemed like an eternity, but at last a puppy appeared. We expected it to be stillborn, so you can imagine the look on our faces when it moved. Yes, it moved. We helped Abby with the cord, dried off the puppy, hugged each other and cried. Then Bob went off to get the video camera.

Sadie, sweet Sadie was a scruffy looking terrier mix who was one of the most loving moms. She had eight puppies, which looked to be boxer mix. She was very attentive, never leaving her babes. She had one of the sweetest faces, which I guess is why she was one of the lucky moms who got adopted quickly.

Shorty was a beagle mix, whom we named based on her physical appearance. Her little legs were so short, and when you added her big belly and sagging milk filled nipples, there wasn't much ground clearance. She was the first mom at my house that lost a pup. She had a baby with a hair lip and it was not able to suck, so the inevitable end was that the pup expired. As hard as she tried, and as hard as we hoped, the end could not be changed. That was when I realized that there is a higher being who oversees what happens, and we must accept and learn from the experience.

One of the most memorable moms was an Akita mix named Dolly. I got a call late at night. The shelter had been informed about a litter of newborns. The story unfolded that Dolly had been abandoned on a porch after her owners moved. She birthed her puppies, and went about the business of being a mom. A neighbor noticed the babies and called the owner, whose response was to return to the house in an intoxicated state and throw the puppies across a creek, leaving Dolly chained to the porch. Luckily, the neighbor called the shelter and the humane officer came to investigate. They retrieved the puppies and reunited them with Dolly. She was, of course, happy to have her babies back, but she was also very guarded about humans. She attempted to bite the officer.

Finally everyone was gathered together and that was when I got the call. It didn't take but 30 seconds to say "Yes". Then 30 seconds later, I was wondering what I had agreed to. There were numerous scenarios passing through my mind as I drove to meet the family. What if she was totally possessive about the babies and wouldn't let me near. What if she attacked me to defend her babies? What if...

I met the officer at the shelter in the parking lot. With some diversion, we transferred everyone to my car. I got home, cautiously picked up and placed one puppy in the kennel area and waited for Dolly to go inside, so that I could transfer the rest. Simple! No growls. No hostile behavior. I was so proud of myself, but most of all, I admired Dolly. Then the thought occurred to me--What was I going to do in 4 hours when I needed to walk her. How was I going to get her OUT of the cage and away form her babies?

This is where the miracle of trust came into play. Somehow, she knew that I only wanted to help, and that I was not another human threat. Dolly was transformed before my eyes. She was gentle, docile, and gave no indication of hostility. She allowed me to put the lead on her collar and we went for a walk. When we returned, she counted her puppies and settled in for the night. At no point did she show any fear or aggressive behavior. They instinctively trusted us as we helped.

Dolly's puppies were one of my favorite litters. As I said, she was an Akita mix so, unlike all the shorthaired labs in the past, they grew to be rolly polly balls of fur. And boy, were they ever-large balls of fur! Their weight at four weeks superseded most of the previous pups at eight weeks. We would open the gate and it would be like a stampede of buffalo. Everything in their path was destroyed. They frolicked in the sun, investigated the flowerbeds, the trees, and all the wonders of the outdoors. And they particularly enjoyed the mud! Puppies, you've got to wonder what goes through their minds! And you've got to love them!

China was the mom with the smallest liter. Only two pups. What happened here? There were always at least eight. She was a white Sharpei mix, and as destiny would have it, one was black and the other white. And oh my, what faces! Little wrinkled mugshots. They must have been the cutest. China had the luxury of raising her pups inside my basement. We set the kennel in a warm spot, and gave her a step stool so she could easily get out as she started to wean. It worked well for China, however the cats weren't too happy as this was their territory.

Sandy was a mottled gray, white, and black hound. Most of our foster pups were black lab mixes, so when we got colors, it was exciting. These puppies were absolutely gorgeous. There were eight of them. Most looked like mom, except for one who looked like a little Rottweiler (Dad, I guess). After five weeks, one of them got ill. After a trip to the vets, including a stay in the incubator, he expired. The next day, the same thing happened. The next day, the same thing. Until only one remained--the tough looking rottweiler guy. As I stated before, I believe in a higher being and for some reason this guy was to overcome the obstacles. We named him Brutus and gave him roam of the spare bedroom. He decided to sleep in the closet. It was so much fun to come home, open the door, call his name, and out he would RUN. The toughest little guy beat the odds and became the biggest tough guy.

Hannah Banana was the last of the moms. She's a big girl with a beautiful black flowing coat. My guess is that she is part Newfoundland. She had a litter of nine, eight black and one yellow (yeah, finally a blonde). She was a young mom, and was very frightened. It took a little coaxing, and a lot of exhaustion to finally get her to relax enough to let her pups nurse. During the first week something just didn't seem right. I had to work, so in a panic I called my friends Harriet and Denny and asked if they take her to the vets. Now, you must realize that only the best of friends would come to your house when you are not at home, and load up their car with a large dog and a basket of puppies. And the best of friends they are! And once again, trust came to light, and Hannah was a perfect lady. No aggression, just a secure feeling for all. As it turned out everyone was fine and life went on. The pups got adopted and Hannah went back to the shelter. I guess because of her size no one adopted her. Months passed and when Christmas Eve arrived, I went back and got her. She stayed with me for a couple of years. I was relentless about asking everyone who mentioned wanting a dog to please consider Hannah. My doctor thought about it, and sent his nanny with her dog, but the chemistry wasn't there. I went to the infamous animal Halloween pageant, and got on stage to ask someone/anyone to find enough love in their heart to give Hannah the home she deserved. Nothing came of that display except public embarrassment for myself. But once again, I would realize that a higher being would intervene. My sister knew of a widow who needed a companion. Hannah and I went to meet her and it was a perfect match. It had taken over two years, but it was worth the wait. Hannah took over the couch, the bed, and Mary Lou's heart. And what a great home. When Mary Lou goes to work, Hannah goes next door to her daughter's and plays with the kids. You can't ask for more love than that.

We fostered for over four years, and each memory is precious. The rewards are endless. There is nothing better than puppy breath and lying on the floor with a litter running all over you, tugging and chewing their way to your heart.

The Shelters

M y first recollection of an animal shelter was when I was a child. We had many pets, and I can remember that the "pound" was a place of disposal, rather than a place to initiate looking for a pet. Pets always just showed up since we lived in a rural area.

I had several siblings, but I was closest in age to my sister Claudia. She was a frail child, and I was a tomboy type, so I guess that I was viewed as the stronger. At any rate, I was always "chosen" to go with my mom when we decided to take a pet to the pound. I remember going inside, being given a brief moment to say goodbye, and then the pet would disappear behind the door. Never to be seen again.

When I graduated from college, I inherited MY first pet. Webster was an Old English Sheepdog who was discarded from a pet store because he had mange. Since the condition was treatable, the consulting vet decided to find a home for him, rather than destroying him. I was lucky enough to talk my landlord into letting me have this "miniature version" of a sheepdog (Good thing he was still a puppy). We went through the puppy process--barricades, training classes, neutering, and spending a lot of time together. He became a trusted friend going everywhere with me, my constant companion. We went to the local park daily. He occasionally wandered, but I would always find him on a blanket with someone who had a basket of food, or at least a couple of kids to amuse him.

However, one day he actually did stray away. I couldn't find him. It was late in the evening and the panic set in. I slept the best I could, awakening several times to look for him, but to no avail. The next morning I was torn between staying home to wait for a call, or canvas the area and keep looking. I placed flyers on the telephone poles (I lived in the city at this point) and called the shelters. I was informed that I had to visit the shelters. What an experience! The cages were overcrowded, the dogs barking, and the anxiety level was at the breaking point. It was horrible enough to be in such a desperate state of mind, but then to have to look at all the unwanted dogs and cats was adding insult to injury. I couldn't imagine my Webby having spent the night here, but the alternatives may have been worse. Needless to say, it was hard to see through the tears. Eventually I went back to my apartment. A couple of hours later, I received a phone call. Someone had called the shelter to report a dog that they found, and the shelter called me with the good news. It turned out that Webby had found a couple of young boys to tag along with. Unbeknownst to them, they took him home because their neighbor had a shaggy dog, and they thought that it was theirs. OOPS! Wrong gender. I guess young boys don't investigate such things. Anyway, Webby spent the night in a warm, cozy house with Molly---good thing we did that neutering.

Years past and again I would visit the shelters. But now it would entail a much happier experience. Perhaps I needed to purge the old memories, and if so, I must admit it worked. We went looking for a dog and found Freckles. A very nervous German shorhaired pointer, but a very loyal and loving companion. It was such a good feeling to rescue a soul from the constant barking and cramped quarters, and to offer a new life.

I then got involved, along with Bob in fostering. We were called upon when the shelter had a pregnant female, and we would foster the moms and puppies for 8 weeks. What a challenge! And what a rewarding experience! There is nothing better than lying on the floor and being covered with puppies! But then the day would come when they had to be returned. The trip to surrender them was always very hard, but we also knew they were going to be adopted, and hopefully they would be with loving families.

I have found that shelters come in all sizes and types, and exhibit varying conditions. Some are No Kill. Others are based only with fostering animals in homes. Some organizations work mainly with educating, while others focus on neutering as a means of controlling the population of the homeless. But all share a dedication to giving the animals a better life. What that better life consists of becomes a debate that sometimes is hard to accept. It is sometimes hard to justify shelters that accept all strays and are No Kill, because they tend to become a collection of hostile snarling dogs. But then my perspective changes when I remember the statement of my friend, Sarah who volunteered at a local shelter. She said that she always knew when it was Thursday, because she could smell the odor left from the euthanizations.

I guess this is the point where I would ask that my journey would possibly become your journey also. If you have some time and some love, and would like to make a difference, please considering volunteering.

Other's Peoples Journeys

A Bag of Apples

I happened to be in the grocery market one day and a
gentleman behind me only had a bag of apples. Since I had
a cart full I invited him to go ahead of me. He thanked me
and said he had to run in to get a bag of apples for his dog.
I thought this strange so I asked him why. He proceeded to
tell me about his dog that he has had for fifteen years, the fact
that she is now blind and having a hard time getting around.
He has to take her outside to do her business but he doesn't
mind. She has been a faithful friend for all these years. Then
he told me that she loves baked apples. So once a week he
goes and gets her a bag. This happened to be in the middle of
the winter so she had to settle for store bought apples. There
is a local orchard and she happens to like the granny smith
apples from that place, but she will have to wait until late
summer for that treat. The gentleman purchased his apples
and we exchanged good-byes. Watching him walk out the
door brought a smile to my face just knowing the love they
both have for one another.

Apache

In April of 2003 Nancy and I happened to be on a trip in the Philadelphia area. We had just gotten off the Pennsylvania Turnpike near the town of Willowlane, Pennsylvania. After coming to a stop at a red light we noticed a Chevrolet Silverado truck directly in front of us. What made this truck so special was an etching on the back glass of the truck. It read as follows:

In Loving Memory
Of my dog
Apache
1/18/1996 - 4/17/2003

I wanted so badly to talk to this gentleman, but were sort of lost in a hurry and it was pouring down rain. But I never forgot that memorial. That's the kind of love that our pets bring out in all of us no matter how we choose to express it.

The Ultimate Sacrifice

T his story just took place a couple of days ago. I met the person I'm writing about; he is a friend of a friend. It's truly a very sad tale, but one that must be told and it will take some time for this to sink in, as it did me. A few days after a very bad storm, this man went out into his backyard to clear a tree that was dead and threatened to topple on his house. It was a very large tree, over forty feet high and five feet round. He began by trimming off some of the bad branches. His dog always was by his side and he thought of him as his child. He was married but had no children, only his loving dog. The dog had been plagued with bad hips. He was a black lab and he even had taken him to Ohio State University School of Veterinary Medicine to see if they could help him.

The dog had real trouble getting up once he lay down and often had to have help. While he was cutting this tree the wind started to gain in intensity. All of a sudden he could hear the tree cracking and it started to blow over. It was falling in the direction of his beloved dog, so the man ran to save him from the tree. Realizing that he would not be able to get him out of the way in time, he dove on top of the dog and the tree landed on top of him killing the man instantly. Neighbors seeing what had happened ran and quickly dragged the tree off of him. They pulled him over, called for an ambulance and someone grabbed the dog and drove him to the local veterinarian. The dog is going to be okay. His owner's love made sure of that.

Epilogue

This brings us not to the end of our journeys, but to where our journeys have led us so far. It has been an extremely interesting one for me. As Nancy likes to put it, a never-ending learning experience. All I know is that the animals that have come into my life for no more than a brief moment I will cherish and always remember. I don't look at it is as if they were taken from me too soon. Rather I feel that I was allowed to know them for however long that time was meant to be. Just writing this reminds me that one day I was washing my car. A little dark haired dog came up to me. He looked tired and thirsty. I grabbed a bowl from the garage and gave him a drink. I ran upstairs to get him some food, as he was probably hungry. I couldn't have been gone for more than two minutes, but when I returned he was already gone. I just kind of smiled, and wished him well on his journey. I wanted to believe that he had been separated from his family and was trying his best to get home.

It's really all we can do to believe what goes on in the minds of animals. Unfortunately, we aren't able to talk to them as I'm talking to you right now. I really think that was by design. To believe in our minds of how we love them and how they love us. We would all be put in straight jackets if a camera were put on us when we are alone with our loved ones. It's like believing in Santa Claus and you then you find out that he doesn't exist but wouldn't the world be a better place if he really did.

There are many organizations out there trying to do what they feel is the right thing to do. Many people believe that animals have souls. If that is true we keeping them as pets is wrong. So we deal with it in our own way. Except for those who are hurting and abusing them, who's to say who is right?

I hope that we have entertained, educated and made you think in the writing of this book. For me, when I got involved with the Humane Society in whelping the mother dogs I finally felt a sense of worth. The joy and pain I received in that undertaking made me realize that if we all did one unselfish deed towards animals that many of the problems facing them and the world would be that much closer to being resolved. Contact your local shelters and talk with them about volunteering, even an hour a week will help. If I can convey any message that it would be SPAY AND NEUTER! Three words could never be more important to the animal world. There are so many unwanted animals and only so much space to keep them. For all the Kodis', Hobos', and Rogers' of the world, please just take a moment to tell them you love them.

Quotable Quotes

Don't accept you dog's admiration as
conclusive evidence that you are wonderful
---Ann Landers

If there are no dogs in Heaven,
then when I die I want to go where they went
---Will Rogers

The average dog is a nicer person than the average person
---Andy Rooney

I wonder if other dogs think poodles
are members of a weird religious cult
---Rita Rudner

If your dog is fat, you aren't getting enough exercise
---Unknown

Women and cats will do as they please,
and men and dogs should relax and get used to the idea
---Robert A Heinlein

If you pick up a starving dog and make him
prosperous, he will not bite you;
that is the principal difference between a dog and man
--Mark Twain

You can say any foolish thing to a dog, and the dog will give
you a look that says, "Wow, you're right! I never would've
thought of that!"
---Dave Barry

Dogs are not our whole life, but they make our lives whole
---Roger Caras

There is no psychiatrist in the world like a puppy licking
your face
--Ben Williams

If you think dogs can't count, try putting three dog biscuits
in your pocket and then give him only two of them
---Phil Pastoret

And the final quotable quote, oddly
from an unknown four year old little boy.
What was it that W.C Fields said about children and animals?

The family of a four-year-old boy was sitting around talking after the death of their family dog. Someone asked why dogs didn't live as long as people. After a short period of time the little boy chimed in with this response:

"I know why. People are born so that they can learn how to live a good life, like loving everybody all the time and being nice, right? Well, dogs already know how to do that, so they don't have to stay as long"

Hope

Just as we thought that the book was finished something happened that I feel I should share with you. Kodi has been in failing health for some time now. He has a problem walking and we felt he was in a lot of discomfort. One-day Nancy called me and asked me to come to talk about the situation. She felt it was time for him to be put to sleep. That we had exhausted all of our options and it was wrong to keep him alive for our selfish needs.

This was a very emotional time for both of us. Kodi has been with us so long and has meant so much to us that this was probably one of the hardest decisions either of us had to make. We both sat on the floor with him and loved him. We decided to call the vet to make the appointment for the following week.

As fate would have it, before we made the appointment, Nancy found an article in the local newspaper about a woman who opened a pet physical therapy office. The article explained her methods, which were primarily massage and hydrotherapy. We were interested, and made an appointment for an evaluation.

The owner, Robin Moore is certified in massage therapy. We met her and she fully explained the procedure. Robin felt that she could help Kodi and stressed that we should also continue to follow up with his veterinarian. This type of therapy is to augment other veterinary practices.

We made appointments for Robin to come to the house to do the therapy so that Kodi would not be inconvenienced by the ride. As we drove home we agreed that Robin was great, and we were hopeful for Kodi. After his first treatment, he was walking around like a puppy. It was amazing to see the difference in him. He was standing straight and walking with a fast gate. His recovery has been somewhat up and down, and we are going to try the hydrotherapy next week. We are encouraged by his progress. The final result may be in fact that Kodi will either pass away or have to be put to sleep. But the HOPE that Robin has given us was worth everything, and the little longer we are able to spend with him is priceless. I know that when that fateful day does come that Kodi will be able to run and play in the fields like he used to do.

A few months later Nancy called to tell me that she and Kodi went for a walk down the driveway. This was significant because up to this point he had a hard time just walking around the house. They had taken many such walks in his younger days, and it was a significant breakthrough that he was able to go the distance.

However, the elation was short lived. I went out in the morning to feed Kodi and Licorice, as Nancy had to work late. Kodi seemed to be having a pretty hard time getting around. Also, he didn't eat all of his food even though I hand fed him. He tried, but just dropped it to the floor. I left that morning only to find out that it would be the last time I would see him alive. When Nancy arrived home, she found him dead on the patio. She called me and I rushed over to the farm. My mind was racing with the thoughts of seeing him. I found Nancy, with Kodi, on the deck. I immediately broke down and then walked toward him and touched his head. We sat and cried, and then proceeded to bury him. We decided to place him in the flower garden in the back yard so that Nancy could see his resting-place from the kitchen window. We wrapped him appropriately and started to dig. When it was time to place him we both carried him to his resting-place. Placing the first shovel of dirt was probably the hardest thing I have ever done. It was at that point that I realized that he was really gone and I would never see him again. I truly had to fight the temptation of not burying him. When he was finally laid to rest I spent the longest time just sitting next to him. I told Nancy that this was the most painful thing I've ever had to endure.

That night I went to Nancy's to let the dogs out while she worked. Driving over I realized that this would be the first time in fourteen years that I would walk into her house and not see Kodi there. When I arrived it was unusually quiet. As I walked inside it seemed strange almost like I had entered a different house. There was no Kodi to greet me. I let the dogs' back into the house and gave each of them a milk bone but this time instead of getting out six, I only needed five. As I turned out the lights and shut the door that strange quiet was still evident. Goodbye my little boy. I will truly miss you

The Rewards

I keep saying that it was one of the most rewarding moments in time in my life and it's absolutely true. You often wonder what you are put on this earth for. Is one of your children going to be president? Will you invent a cure for a terrible disease? Or will you in some small way without many people knowing it, touch and change their lives? An animal brings so much love and joy into our lives that I feel we take that for granted. For many of us, it's not until that loved one passes that we come to realize how much they meant to us and how much we depended on them for our very being.

Do I believe in love at first sight? Yes, I believe I do. I know how I've felt myself not only with animals, but also with people. There is a connection that you can't describe but you know it is right. I've seen it many times in the eyes of people when they come to the shelter looking for a pet. And what is it that drives us to want an animal? Certainly they are more undertaking than I think we realize. Especially, when it's the first time someone has ever had a pet as a companion. We have dozens of reasons why we say we want a pet, but in reality I believe there is a void left from our interactions with people.

I just wish that everyone would realize that void and fill it with an animal. Think back to when you first took your pet home and what a challenge it was making the adjustment for both of you. Then soon that challenge was forgotten and the seeming tasks that we first undertook were soon looked upon as a normal part of our lives.

Blue Creek Jasper
1986-2007

Scooter
The Journey Begins Again.

www.ingramcontent.com/pod-product-compliance
Lightning Source LLC
Chambersburg PA
CBHW020243290526
45784CB00003B/1091